DISCOVERING THE UNITED STATES

Virginia

BY CANDICE RANSOM

An Imprint of Abdo Publishing
abdobooks.com

abdobooks.com

Published by Abdo Publishing, a division of ABDO, PO Box 398166, Minneapolis, Minnesota 55439.

Printed in China.
052024
092024

Cover Photo: iStockphoto
Interior Photos: Jon Marc Lyttle/Shutterstock Images, 4–5; Bonnie Taylor Barry/Shutterstock Images, 7 (top left); J. K. Laws/Shutterstock Images, 7 (top right); Mary Terriberry/Shutterstock Images, 7 (bottom left); Aruni Udeshika/Shutterstock Images, 7 (bottom right); Douglas Rissing/E+/Getty Images, 9; Robert H. Ellis/Shutterstock Images, 10; Kim Kelley-Wagner/Shutterstock Images, 12–13; Buyenlarge/Archive Photos/Getty Images, 14; Travel/Interfoto/Alamy, 17; Shutterstock Images, 18, 24, 29 (bottom); Sean Pavone/Shutterstock Images, 20–21, 28 (bottom); Jay Yuan/Shutterstock Images, 22; M. Bell/Moment/Getty Images, 23; L. Toshio Kishiyama/Moment/Getty Images, 26; Shackleford Photography/Shutterstock Images, 28 (top left); Red Line Editorial, 28 (top right), 29 (top)

Editor: Laura Stickney
Series Designer: Katharine Hale

Library of Congress Control Number: 2023949375

Publisher's Cataloging-in-Publication Data

Names: Ransom, Candice, author.
Title: Virginia / by Candice Ransom
Description: Minneapolis, Minnesota: Abdo Publishing, 2025 | Series: Discovering the United States | Includes online resources and index.
Identifiers: ISBN 9781098294175 (lib. bdg.) | ISBN 9798384913443 (ebook)
Subjects: LCSH: U.S. states--Juvenile literature. | Virginia--History--Juvenile literature. | Southeastern States--Juvenile literature. | Physical geography--United States--Juvenile literature.
Classification: DDC 973--dc23

All population data taken from:
"Estimates of Population by Sex, Race, and Hispanic Origin: April 1, 2020 to July 1, 2022." *US Census Bureau, Population Division*, June 2023, census.gov.

CONTENTS

On Jamestown Island, visitors can explore the site of the Jamestown colony. They can take tours, see old buildings, and learn about new discoveries.

CHAPTER 1

The Jamestown Colony

It was May 14, 1607. Three ships from England arrived at an island in the James River. This was in what is now the state of Virginia. The ships carried 104 men and boys. The new settlers built a fort on the island. They named their **colony** Jamestown.

American Indians had been living in the area for a long time. At first, the Powhatan people traded goods with the settlers. But the settlers ran out of food. They started fighting with the Powhatan for food. Some settlers became sick. Many of them died.

Jamestown Discoveries

Jamestown was home to James Fort. For many years, people believed that the fort had been washed away by the James River. William Kelso is an **archaeologist**. He studies old buildings to learn about Virginia's past. In 1994, Kelso began digging on Jamestown Island. He found parts of the old fort. Kelso and his team have uncovered 3 million items. These include pottery pieces, parts of swords, and coins.

Virginia Facts

DATE OF STATEHOOD
June 25, 1788

CAPITAL
Richmond

POPULATION
8,683,619

AREA
42,775 square miles
(110,787 sq km)

STATE BIRD

Northern cardinal

STATE TREE

American dogwood

STATE FLOWER

American dogwood

STATE DOG

American foxhound

Each US state has a different population, size, and capital city. States also have state symbols.

In 1612, settler John Rolfe planted tobacco. He sent the crop back to England. The English had been buying tobacco from Spain. But the tobacco from Jamestown tasted different.

The English king wanted the Jamestown settlers to plant more of the crop. Many people in England began buying tobacco from the colony. This helped Jamestown earn money to survive.

The Jamestown colony lasted for almost 100 years. It was the first successful English community in what would later become the United States. Today, people can visit the site of the colony on Jamestown Island in Virginia.

Virginia's Land

Virginia is in the US region called the South. The state borders Maryland to the north and northeast. West Virginia and Kentucky lie to the west. To the south are North Carolina and Tennessee. Chesapeake **Bay** divides part of

At Great Falls National Park, people can see waterfalls and rapids along the Potomac River. Some people kayak down the river.

eastern Virginia from the rest of the state. The state's eastern coast borders the Atlantic Ocean.

Virginia's land includes beaches, marshes, and forests. Black bears live in the Blue Ridge Mountains. Eagles fly over the James River.

In the fall, people can drive along the Blue Ridge Parkway to see Virginia's autumn colors.

The Potomac River divides Virginia and Maryland. It flows into Chesapeake Bay.

Climate

Virginia has four seasons. The climate is usually humid. In the spring, dogwood trees bloom. Summers are long and hot. In the fall, trees have colorful leaves. Winters in much of Virginia are mild. But heavy snow falls in the western mountains.

Explore Online

Visit the website below. Does it give any new information about Virginia that wasn't in Chapter One?

Virginia

abdocorelibrary.com/discovering-virginia

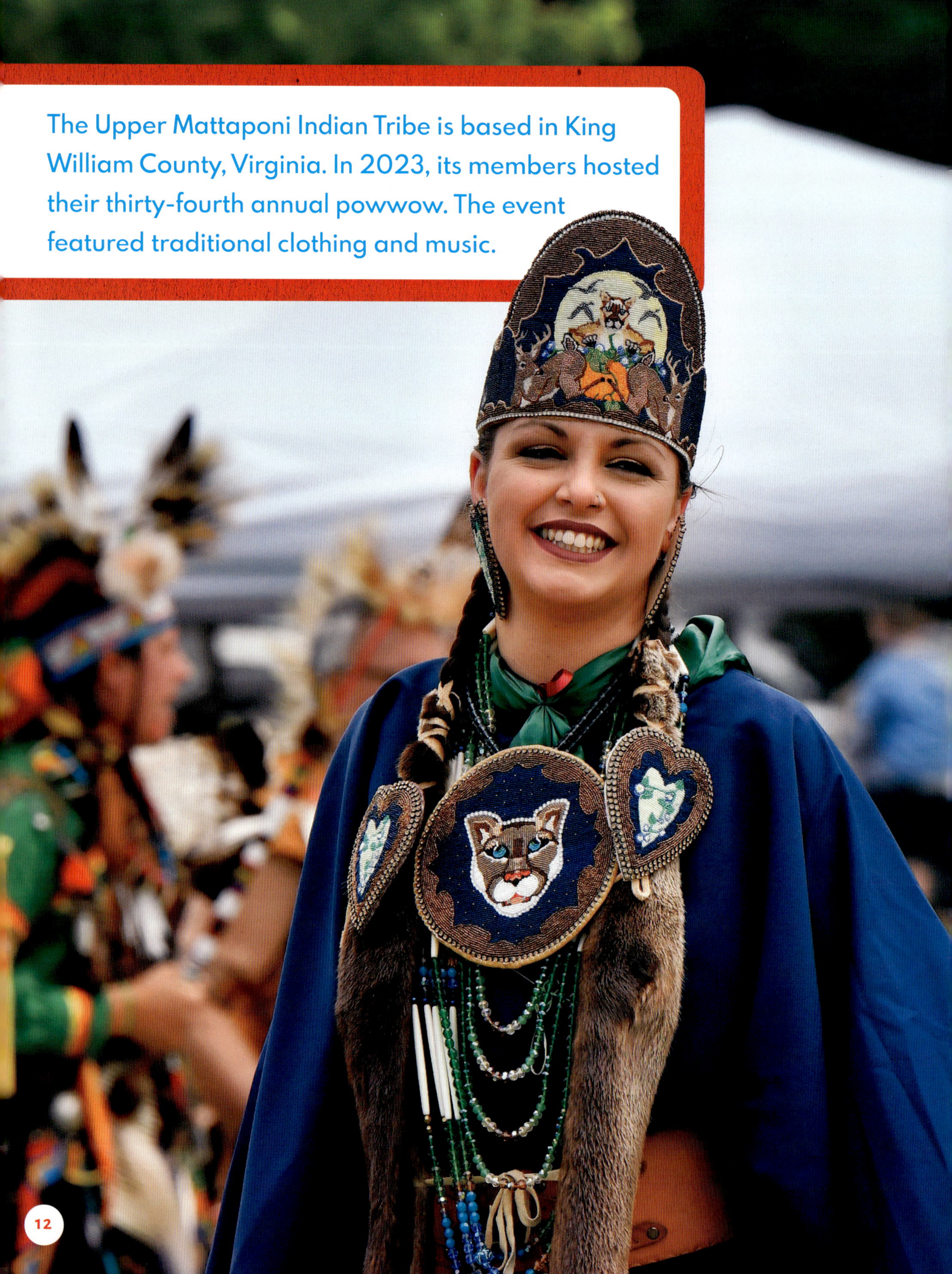

The Upper Mattaponi Indian Tribe is based in King William County, Virginia. In 2023, its members hosted their thirty-fourth annual powwow. The event featured traditional clothing and music.

The People of Virginia

American Indians lived in Virginia as early as 18,000 years ago. Early American Indians lived in villages. Many hunted animals and grew crops. By the early 1600s, many nations formed the Powhatan **Confederation**.

In 1860, enslaved Black people made up one-third of Virginia's population. At the time, Virginia had more enslaved people than any other state.

People in this group spoke several languages, including Algonquian.

Immigration

The first English settlers arrived in Virginia in 1607. In 1619, a ship carrying enslaved people from Africa landed near Jamestown. Europeans had captured these people from their homeland. During the 1700s and 1800s, more Europeans and enslaved Africans arrived.

German, Scottish, and Irish immigrants also settled in Virginia.

Today, Virginia's population is about 60 percent white. It is 20 percent Black and 10 percent Hispanic or Latino. About 7 percent of Virginians are Asian, and less than 1 percent are American Indian. The state's government officially recognizes 11 American Indian nations.

Mother of Presidents

Virginia is the birthplace of more US presidents than any other state. For this reason, Virginia is often called the Mother of Presidents. The presidents from the state are George Washington, Thomas Jefferson, James Madison, James Monroe, William Henry Harrison, John Tyler, Zachary Taylor, and Woodrow Wilson.

These include the Mattaponi, Pamunkey, and Chickahominy.

Culture

Music is a big part of Virginia's culture. Many music styles developed around the Appalachian Mountains. They include folk, bluegrass, and country music. People can learn about Virginia's music history by following the Crooked Road trail. It connects music history sites.

Virginia is also known for several traditional foods. Seafoods such as trout and blue crab are popular. The state's mild climate is great for growing apples too. Southern Virginia is known for ham and peanuts.

The Crooked Road driving trail is 330 miles (531 km) long. Music venues, museums, and roadside exhibits lie along the road.

Industry

Virginia has several major industries. Many people have technology jobs. The Amazon company's **headquarters** opened in Arlington in 2023.

Other Virginians have government jobs. The state is home to Naval Station Norfolk, a US naval base. Others work at the Pentagon.

Virginia's state flag features a female warrior holding a spear and sword. She stands over a fallen king.

That is the headquarters of the US Department of Defense. Tourism is another big industry in the state. Many tourists visit Virginia's parks and historical sites.

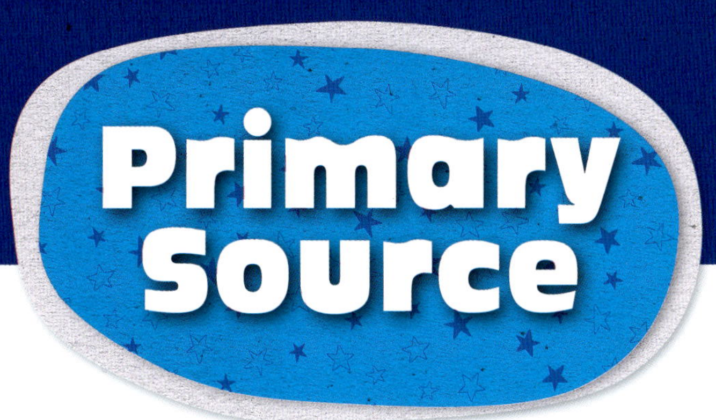

Virginia farmer Elisha Barnes grows peanuts without using any modern machinery. In an interview, Barnes said:

> I want to maintain something so that generations now and generations to come see just a snippet of what used to be normal living on a country farm.

Source: Marisa Marsey. "Local Peanut Farmer's 'Shocking' Methods." *Coastal Virginia Magazine*, 1 Sept. 2022, coastalvirginiamag.com. Accessed 26 Oct. 2023.

What's the Big Idea?

What is this quote's main idea? Explain how the main idea is supported by details.

Downtown Richmond is home to many historic buildings and neighborhoods. The city is known for its scenic riverfront area.

CHAPTER 3

Places in Virginia

The capital of Virginia is Richmond. It is located on the James River. The city of Virginia Beach is on the state's southeastern coast. It is the state's largest and most populous city. The county of Arlington is located near Washington, DC.

Chincoteague National Wildlife Refuge is one of the only places where Chincoteague ponies live. These wild ponies have shaggy fur and eat marsh grasses.

The state also has two **reservations**. Both are in eastern Virginia. The Pamunkey and Mattaponi nations have land there.

Parks

Virginia has 42 state parks and 22 national parks. Shenandoah National Park is located in the Blue Ridge Mountains. People can hike and camp there.

Natural Bridge was carved out of rock by water from a creek. Today, visitors can walk along a trail that goes under the bridge.

Chincoteague National Wildlife Refuge includes more than 14,000 acres (5,670 ha) of beaches and marshes. It is home to many animals, including wild ponies. At Natural Bridge State Park, visitors can see a rock bridge. It is 215 feet (65.5 m) tall and 500 million years old.

George Washington lived at Mount Vernon from 1754 to 1799. He designed parts of the mansion.

Landmarks

One famous Virginia landmark is Mount Vernon. It was the home of President George Washington. Visitors can tour the house and gardens. They can also see Washington's grave. In Charlottesville, people can visit Monticello, the home of President Thomas Jefferson. It is a National Historic Landmark.

Arlington is home to Arlington National Cemetery. Many famous people are buried there. They include President John F. Kennedy and US Supreme Court Justice Ruth Bader Ginsburg.

The College of William and Mary

In 1693, the College of William and Mary opened in Williamsburg. It is the country's second-oldest college. US presidents Thomas Jefferson, James Monroe, and John Tyler attended the college. In Fall 2022, more than 6,700 undergraduate students were enrolled in the school.

In Colonial Williamsburg, visitors can ride through the streets in horse-drawn carriages.

Another popular site is Colonial Williamsburg. People can explore historical buildings and learn about early life in Virginia. They can watch costumed actors make tools or weave cloth. They can also eat peanut soup at an old **inn**.

Virginia is full of amazing sights and experiences. People can learn about history at Jamestown or Mount Vernon. They can explore and see wildlife at the state's many parks. All kinds of adventures await in Virginia.

Further Evidence

Look at the website below, which contains a map of Virginia's state parks. Does it give any new evidence to support Chapter Three?

Virginia State Parks: Map

abdocorelibrary.com/discovering-virginia

State Map

Arlington National Cemetery

Richmond

Virginia: The Old Dominion State

N
W
E
S
Ohio
Maryland
Potomac River
Washington, DC
Shenandoah River
West Virginia
Arlington National Cemetery
The Pentagon
Mount Vernon
Chincoteague National Wildlife Refuge
Shenandoah National Park
Chesapeake Bay
Kentucky
Monticello
Williamsburg
James River
Richmond
Norfolk
Natural Bridge State Park
Jamestown Settlement
Virginia Beach
Tennessee
North Carolina
Atlantic Ocean

Mount Vernon

Glossary

archaeologist
a scientist who studies the history of humans by discovering human-made objects

bay
a small body of water connected to an ocean or lake

colony
an area that is controlled by another country

confederation
an alliance formed by multiple nations or groups

headquarters
the main office of an organization

inn
a public house that provides lodging and food for travelers

reservations
lands set aside by a government for a specific group of people

Online Resources

To learn more about Virginia, visit our free resource websites below.

Visit **abdocorelibrary.com** or scan this QR code for free Common Core resources for teachers and students, including vetted activities, multimedia, and booklinks, for deeper subject comprehension.

Visit **abdobooklinks.com** or scan this QR code for free additional online weblinks for further learning. These links are routinely monitored and updated to provide the most current information available.

Learn More

Payne, Stefanie. *The National Parks.* DK, 2020.

Tieck, Sarah. *Virginia.* Abdo, 2020.

Trusiani, Lisa. *The Story of George Washington.* Rockridge, 2020.

Index

About the Author

Candice Ransom is an author. Her family has lived in Virginia for eleven generations.